The Small Cap Secrets of Wall Street

ANONYMOUS

ISBN-13: 978-0615994130
ISBN-10: 061599413X

DISCLAIMER

CONTENTS

ACKNOWLEDGMENTS

THE GREAT THING about being anonymous is that there's no need to thank anyone. Make your own success!

INTRODUCTION

I'D LIKE TO THANK Robert Frost for urging us all to follow "the path less traveled by." I was once an investor of above-average skill, working on Wall Street, and making a great living at it. But, I veered off, "and that has made all the difference."

Since deciding to follow the path less traveled, I've made a small fortune in small caps. They've allowed me to have the life I always wanted to have.

I'm not the first to figure out that small caps can be great investments with significant returns, but I'm one of the only brazen enough to throw elitism to the wind and share my secrets to success.

My aim is to give you the knowledge, guidance, and *chutzpah* you need to start investing in small caps—and to make big money doing it.

I can't say that small cap investing is easy; it isn't. But, I will say that it's challenging with tremendous rewards—financial and personal—if you're willing to learn the rules, follow them persistently, and break them whenever necessary.

I'll try to set forth my ideas as plainly as possible. I'll do my best to explain the whole process in non-financial language. I want to spare you the typical "investment-book" experience. Who said reading a book about investing had to be complicated?

A CAP IS A CAP... OR IS IT?

BEFORE WE BEGIN, have you read the Disclaimer included with this book? If not, please take a moment to do so now. *Do not continue reading if you have yet to read the Disclaimer.*

So, what exactly are small caps?

It's simple, really. *Cap* is short for "market capitalization," which means the total value of a company. It's what you get if you multiply the number of outstanding shares of a company by the share price. That's it.

A *small cap* is a publicly traded company with a market capitalization between $300 million and $2 billion. A *micro cap* is even smaller, with a market capitalization between $50 million to $300 million.

Small caps and micro caps are not defined in terms of share price.

Penny stocks, however, are. A *penny stock* is defined by the U.S. Securities and Exchange Commission (SEC) as a stock with a share price below $5. Penny stocks may have a bad name—the phrase even sounds negative—but, in many cases they can offer massive returns if bought and sold at the right time. The most savvy small cap investors don't throw away pennies.

It's important to keep in mind that there's a difference between stocks that are worthless and penny stocks poised to break out. With stock, it's all a matter of knowing what to buy and when.

So, when you hear about inexpensive stocks, you could be hearing about a few things:
1. Penny stocks.
2. Small cap and micro cap stocks.
3. Large cap stocks with low share prices.

In this book, I'm using the term "small cap" to cover companies that are small caps, micro caps, or penny stocks, as I defined them on the last page—this will make life easier to use one term for all three. Most companies in this category are just starting out. I'm not including large caps with low share prices because that's an entirely different ball game.

Now that we've dealt with the terminology, let's move on to the question of how small caps operate and why you should, or should not, invest in them.

Let's start with some negatives:
*   In general, small caps have greater risk and higher unpredictability than mid caps and large caps.
*   Small caps poised to break out are harder to hear about and research, since there is generally less information about them.

I won't give you the "every cloud has a silver lining" routine, but I will tell you that each negative listed above has a matching positive—and a powerful positive, at that:
*   First, small caps might be somewhat unpredictable, but they also produce greater returns than mid and large caps. In fact,

small caps are historically the first stocks to rebound during economic recoveries—so, the time to invest is now.

- Second, the fact that small caps are less studied by the "powers-that-be" is a great advantage. This isn't a jab at Wall Street—it's a fact. There is serious money to be made if you know what to buy and when.

Just look at small caps in the context of history…

The story of American business is a story of visionaries—like Henry Ford and Andrew Carnegie—who created corporate empires with very little money. Ford borrowed funds from friends to start the Ford Company. Carnegie worked as a telegraph operator and part-time bond salesman to build U.S. Steel.

American business is a story of huge corporations starting from nothing and taking the world by storm. For example: Dell, Microsoft, Xerox, Hewlett-Packard, Wrigley's, Mattel, Whole Foods, and Coors. The list goes on and on. A huge proportion of today's Fortune 500 companies began on a shoestring.

The fact is that most large, successful, American corporations started out small—and they still do. That's precisely why it pays for smart investors like you to invest in small caps. The great ideas of tomorrow are being hatched in the small cap companies of today.

Over the last few decades, small companies have been playing an increasingly significant role as incubators of innovation. They've been fueling a growing percentage of the research and development that produces breakthroughs and impacts our lives and economics.

In 2006, 24% of the research and development taking place in business was being done by small companies, as opposed to only 4% in 1981. Small companies are inching their way up as the movers and shakers of progress. They are also creating the jobs that will eventually shrink the unemployment rate and revive our economy.

Small caps in particular have created the greatest historical gains in value and growth. The figures are impressive.

More recently—in the four years following the worst bear market since the Great Depression—the success of small caps has been remarkable. The Russell 2000 Index—a small cap benchmark index—rose 24% in 2009.

Despite the crisis of 2008, small caps have outperformed large caps by a large margin. The Russell 2000 Index returned a 9.5% premium over the S&P 500 Index on an annualized basis. The EURO STOXX Small Index outperformed the EURO STOXX 50 Index by almost 12% on an annualized basis.

Small and Large Cap Stocks Historical Returns[1]

	1 Year 2010	5 Years 2006-2010	10 Years 2001-2010	20 Years 1991-2010	50 Years 1961-2010	80 Years 1931-2010
Small Cap Value	34.6	4.8	13.8	15.6	15.3	15.4
Large Cap Value	20.2	-3.7	-0.1	8.2	11.4	11.2
Small Cap Growth	31.8	3.4	3.0	8.2	8.2	10.2
Large Cap Growth	17.6	3.9	-0.4	8.5	8.9	9.4

Annualized Return of Small Cap Indexes

Index	Annualized Return	Standard Deviation
EURO STOXX Small Index	33.7%	17.7%
EURO STOXX 50 Index	22.0%	16.6%
Russell 2000 Index	42.6%	19.8%
S&P 500 Index	33.1%	14.8%
MSCI World Index	29.9%	15.7%

Time Period: 03/2009 – 07/2011

Best Performing Stocks Over A Decade [2]
(9 of 10 are small caps)

Company	10-Year Total Return	Market Cap 10 Years Ago	Business
Monster Beverage (MNST)	21,050%	$35 million	Natural sodas and energy sports drinks
Deckers Outdoors (DECK)	5,210%	$37 million	Casual outdoor footwear
Green Mountain Coffee Roasters (GMCR)	4,140%	$177 million	Specialty coffees
Apple (AAPL)	4,000%	$7.9 billion	Computers and smartphones
Newmarket (NEU)	3,550%	$77 million	Petroleum lubricants and additives

Company	10-Year Total Return	Market Cap 10 Years Ago	Business
Cliffs Natural (CLF)	3,490%	$146 million	Iron ore mining
Southern Copper (SCCO)	3,150%	$956 million	Copper mining
Middleby (MIDD)	3,000%	$46 million	Restaurant equipment
Cal-Maine Foods (CALM)	2,900%	$43 million	Eggs
Quality Systems (SQII)	2,580%	$99 million	Healthcare information software

To download these tables, along with all other tables in this book, packaged as a "go-to" PDF, please visit this webpage: www.smallcapsecrets.com/tables

One reason for the solid outperformance of small caps over large caps since 2008 is that expanding financial policies have produced an environment that supports small caps. During this time, large caps have had to cut costs to increase their available cash. At the same time, many large caps have acquired small caps, sending prices soaring.

This trend of outperformance is likely to continue, given that Federal Reserve Chairman Ben Bernanke has committed himself to keeping interest rates at the current levels (which are really low) for at least two years.

Plus, small caps hold several advantages over large caps. The following facts speaks for themselves:

1. Small cap organizations are more streamlined.
2. They have less red tape to contend with.
3. Even more importantly, they "fly under the radar." Meaning, they remain relatively unnoticed until investors discover them…
4. At which point they increase in value, sometimes by 1,000% or more.

So, why should you invest in small caps?

Because that's where there's real money to be made by confident, tough-minded, investors. Events in 2008 may have scared off the faint-hearted and turned a lot of people sour, but they gave those of us who were bull-headed the chance to cash in on bearish fear.

And, if past recessions are anything to go by, it's the small cappers who will lead the way out.

---

[1] Michael Zhuang, "Small Cap Value: Risk and Returns," *The Investment Fiduciary* (blog), March 29, 2011, http://investment-fiduciary.com/2011/03/29/small-cap-value-risk-and-returns/

[2] Jim Fink, "Buy Small-Cap Stocks Before They Grow Up," *Investing Daily* (blog), February 14, 2012, http://www.investingdaily.com/10884/buy-small-cap-stocks-before-they-grow-up

SIZE INFLUENCES EFFICIENCY

THE *efficient market theory* is often regarded as an essential element of stock market studies. It's rational and has a long academic history. But, like many good theories, it's flawed.

It basically says that all of the publically available information about a given stock is already factored into the share price. To a great extent, this is true for stocks that are heavily studied by analysts and institutions—so, large caps. But, it's not usually true for small caps.

This is a good thing! The lack of information (at least, "official" information) out there when it comes to small caps means it cannot already be factored into share prices. So, there's more room for a clever investor to beat the system. For people who know what to buy, and when, this lack of information is an enormous advantage.

According to the efficient market theory, it's almost impossible to beat the market. However, in the 1980's, researchers started noticing something: they noticed that the number of analysts following a stock could affect its price. Several studies concluded that stocks that are followed by *fewer* analysts have *greater* returns.

Most small caps fall into this category. In fact, many have nobody studying them at all. And, if they do, it's typically only a handful of analysts at most.

This is where the small cap advantage comes into play. Because there is less information and less attention, small caps are more likely to defy the efficient market theory than other stocks. Since information isn't out there, it can't be built into price. So, small caps offer the clever investor—who knows where to find the right information at the right time—a fair likelihood of success.

The Internet has absolutely transformed the nature and availability of that information. There's more information to be had, and it's more accessible than ever before. But, the information—as with everything today—is often mixed in with misinformation. It takes some work to figure out what's true, accurate, and relevant—and what's not. Because of this, the difference between stocks that are highly studied and those that are not is greater than it ever was. This means that if you're feisty and independent, and you know what you're doing (which I'll make sure you do), you're ahead of the game by default. You're positioned to win.

If you think about it, your role as an investor is not that different from a venture capitalist—except that you don't have to invest extreme amounts of money in the companies you've researched. You can be a big fish in the small cap pond.

How do you think I made my money? I studied the small caps no one was looking at, made sure I'd received the best information and alerts, and kept my thoughts to myself.

You can do the same. Your aim, after all, isn't to publish your findings on the small cap companies you follow. It's to study these companies on your own, decide whether to invest, and to make gains for yourself.

I'll teach you my secrets to do this, but do yourself a favor—keep them under your cap!

SMALL ADVANTAGES ARE HUGE

YOU'RE A GO-GETTER. The fact that you're trying to educate yourself about small caps proves it. You've already passed the most important risk test there is—the test of personal comfort. You've faced the fact that there's a certain risk in investing in companies that most people have never heard of, and you're comfortable with it. In fact, you've decided to embrace it

Obviously, you intend to make the right choices—buying and selling the right small caps at the right time. But, to do this, you need to spend some time looking within and pondering what works for you in terms of personal risk tolerance. You need to consider factors like:

1. Your age.
2. Your family needs.
3. Your income.
4. Your assets.
5. Your tax situation.

Think about your age, where you are in your working life—whether you're actively involved in your career, close to retirement, or already retired.

Think about your family—and your obligation to your spouse, your parents, your children, and/or grandchildren. Think about the costs of things like: education, child care, health care, housing, house purchases, vacations, and family events like weddings.

Think about your income, your projected retirement income, and your level of disposable income—and how much you have to "play with."

Think about your assets, and whether you're responsible for mortgages, loans, and credit cards.

Think about your tax situation, how vulnerable you are to an increased tax burden, and how you would handle additional profits and losses.

Think about your knowledge of and your experience in investing, and whether you have (or don't have) a track record.

You need to seriously ponder these issues before you are ready to look at the risk-and-return issues involved in buying and selling small caps. Understand that buying and selling stock is very much like gambling. *Never invest more than you can afford to lose.*

Still with me? Great. So, what's the best way to buy and sell small caps?

First, consider small caps as part of the *equities* portion of your portfolio. Before you make decisions about small caps, you need to decide how much space equities in general will take up in your larger investment portfolio.

Few professionals today believe in a uniform percentage-based allocation for all investment portfolios. Realizing that each investor has different needs and risk tolerance levels, they take a more flexible approach.

Today, asset allocation strategies are based not only by the nature of securities themselves, but on the needs of investors and their tolerance for risk. Risk management has come to play an important part in asset allocation and portfolio planning.

There are two different schools of thought about risk management. The *quantitative school* focuses on the mathematical aspects of risk and return, using correlations, trends, and studies of the historical past as the basis for risk and reward decisions. The *qualitative school*, in contrast, believes in basing these decisions on subjective factors, and focuses on the future rather than the past.

The big fuss over which school is right is irrelevant. You need to look at both and use both. There is no one ideal strategy that works for everybody.

Whether you use a financial planner or plan your portfolio yourself, you need to consider:
1. Your specific goals.
2. Your time frame for reaching those goals.
3. Your current financial and tax situation.
4. Your financial holdings.
5. Your risk tolerance.
6. Your liquidity or cash needs.
7. Any special issues influencing your investment decisions.

You need to pay careful attention to your own investment needs to build the right portfolio.

It's vitally important that you diversify both your overall portfolio and all equities, including small caps, by company, sector, company size, and investment type. I'm talking about spreading risk and

ceNew WWW.SMALLCAPSECRETS.COM

reducing your exposure in such a way that, no matter what is happening in the market, only a portion of your investments will be affected. Bear in mind that diversification is not just a matter of creating profit, but a management tool.

Even though this book is about investing in small caps, purchasing small caps—no matter how diversified they may be—without purchasing other types of equities or fixed income as well, is not smart. Similarly, over-diversification—owning too many stocks, or dealing with too large a mutual fund—is a mistake. You are not likely to beat the market if you overdo it.

It's a mistake to regard equities as a single component of an investment portfolio or to limit yourself to small caps. Experts recommend subdividing your equities into different kinds of stock investments—including a mix of direct ownership of micro cap, small cap, mid cap, and large cap stocks, plus mutual funds, or exchange-traded funds (EFTs). This is crucial to achieving a properly diversified portfolio.

As a small cap investor, you must also think carefully about how you mix your small caps with other categories of stock. You want to reduce risk. It's one of the most important things you can do as an investor.

Then, by learning about the nature of small caps and how they work in conjunction with other asset classes, you'll be able to decide on the role you want small caps to play in your investment life—and your portfolio.

Small caps are riskier than larger caps. But, it's a documented fact that, over time, they generate higher returns. On the whole, they are more volatile than more established stocks. But, according to prevailing portfolio theory, the right mixture of volatile stocks in a portfolio can actually *reduce* risk.

Let's explore a few issues in portfolio theory, starting with what is called the *Capital Asset Pricing Model* (CAPM). According to CAPM, knowing a security's expected return and how it changes with other securities can help determine whether or not you should include it in your investment portfolio. The key to the CAPM model is the concept of the *beta co-efficient*, which is the measure of risk as it relates to the broader market. The higher the *beta* of a portfolio, the higher its return should be. According to a related theory, the *Arbitrage Pricing Theory*, many factors—not just the beta coefficient—affect stock returns.

The debate about different factors that influence the level of return on stocks has brought attention to an important fact: *Small caps behave differently than large caps.*

Some of these differences have to do with issues factored into costs. Some of these differences have to do with who buys and doesn't buy them. For example, huge institutions can't invest in small caps even if they want to, because the numbers of available shares are usually too small for institutional investment. And, most large mutual funds do not handle small caps; if they do, they charge heavily for doing so.

Having briefly touched on some of the differences in the way small and large caps behave, we arrive at the point I'm trying to make: *Since small caps are not widely traded by large institutions, small caps give the individual investor an edge in profiting from their high returns.* This is another huge advantage.

TAKING STOCK

NOW IT'S TIME to do more than talk about investing. Stop for a moment to reflect. What are your aims? What are your expectations? What are your passions?

With these questions percolating in your mind, get out your laptop, tablet, or spiral notebook. Investors, like novelists, should always be ready to jot things down. An investing journal is valuable.

Just start writing down your answers.

Take my advice and do it now; it's worth it. Knowing where you're coming from and where you want to go as an investor is an important part of the process. Do this whenever you need to clear your mind and regain focus. It's just as important as writing down stock tips.

If you want to be successful, you need to be able to brainstorm by yourself. After all, you're someone you know you can trust. You need to keep track of your hunches and your doubts. You need to think for yourself and listen to yourself. If you don't, you'll get emotional, listen to others, second-guess yourself, and make the wrong decisions.

I learned some things from my years in the financial establishment, and I'm willing to share my secrets. But these things will only be useful if you get yourself in gear. They were only useful to me because I listened to myself, no matter what I read and studied.

If you are a newcomer to investing, you may not have experience with the stock market—but you do have instinct and guts. That's enough. I'll teach you the rest.

Before we begin, you need to commit to educating yourself. Aside from this book, you need to start exploring investment websites and financial media. Familiarize yourself with the various kinds of charts investors use. Learn about the SEC, stock exchanges and indexes, the "Pink Sheets," and OTC Bulletin Board (OTCBB). Read as much as you can, so you can learn investment lingo. Peruse the financial pages. Find out what kind of information you need, and what skills you need to acquire or brush up on. Take online tutorials, call brokers, go to the local library, bug your investor-friends.

In fact, there's a lot of additional information at my website: www.smallcapsecrets.com. Sign up for the newsletter!

Once you've committed that you'll do the additional work, open your eyes to the world of publicly traded companies.

First, you'll need to figure out what sources of information about small caps are helpful and legit. You'll need to know where to go to get the latest alerts and press releases on up-and-coming companies.

You'll also want to pay attention to what's going on around you—in the world at large, and right around the corner. Follow the trends. Pay attention to what's happening in medicine, pharmacology, energy, security, and sustainability. What technology is becoming obsolete? What's replacing it? What's going on in the world at large? What are the global trends? What's going on with oil, gold, and other commodities? Preventive security, software, services? And, while you're at it, don't forget the mundane. What's new in lunch box snacks, cat foods, and yoga clothes? Literally, consider anything that you can think of. A great way to get your mind moving is to sign up for newsletters that issue press releases and news alerts at websites specially catering to investor relations for small caps. If you haven't already, sign up for my newsletter at: www.smallcapsecrets.com.

Look around. There are thousands of publicly held stocks to study and ponder. Though you are unlikely to find much analysis, commentary, and advice on promising small caps in the financial media (remember, this is an advantage), there are places where this type of information is available to select groups of people. Since information is reflected in share pricing, it is important to move quickly once information has been released. You need to absorb that information and decide whether to invest before the information gets reflected in share pricing. This is how elite small cappers know what to buy and when. They're the first to receive press releases and alerts, they get their research done fast, and decide whether or not to buy. Since they've bought quickly, before that information has had a chance to be reflected in a small cap's share price, they have the opportunity to cash out on huge gains, while those who didn't receive the information first are left looking at gains that could have been.

Get into the habit of reading (in hard copy or online):
- *The Wall Street Journal* (www.wsj.com).
- *The Economist* (www.economist.com).
- *Financial Times* (www.ft.com).
- *Forbes* (www.forbes.com).
- *Fortune* (www.fortune.com).
- *Businessweek* (www.businessweek.com).

- *Investors' Business Daily* (www.investors.com).
- *Investment News Daily* (www.investmentnews.com).

You can also find investment news practically everywhere on the Internet—from Google Finance and Yahoo! Finance to CNN. For market data, see Reuters (www.reuters.com) and Bloomberg (www.bloomberg.com).

Check out Russell Investments (www.russell.com). The Russell 2000 Index measures the performance of the 2,000 smallest companies in the Russell 2000 Index, and is the benchmark of small caps in the United States. Using this web site, you can monitor small caps in real time.

At INVESTools (www.investools.com) you can access a wide variety of financial newsletters, plus a free digest that provides weekly summaries from newsletters and advisory services. They also have a database of thousands of companies, where you can screen stocks for dozens of variables such as market cap, earnings per share growth, revenue growth, and insider ownership percentages.

For useful online information on industry sectors, you can search Google News for "record earnings." And, of course, there's the SEC website, where you can get the official low-down on publicly-held companies, and download every important filing.

Then there's Investopedia (www. investopedia.com), which has a very useful financial dictionary, tutorials, free newsletters, and even a stock simulator where you can do "fantasy investing."

StockCharts.com (www.stockcharts.com) is a place where you can learn technical analysis quite painlessly. In addition to charts, it offers tutorials that are great for the investor who wants to learn about the various kinds of charts. You can follow the companies you're interested in studying and make customized charts, which you can update on an ongoing basis.

Finally, when dealing with penny stocks, be sure to check OTC Markets for Pink Sheets stocks (www.otcmarkets.com) and the OTC Bulletin Board's website for OTCBB stocks (www.otcbb.com). You'll want to look for the number of outstanding shares, "caveat emptor" or "stop" ratings, the current filing status, state of incorporations, as well as any available news, press information, and additional material.

Not everything you read—especially in the Internet world—is true. You need to be on guard if you expect to learn how small caps function in the larger financial universe.

To download a listing of the previously mentioned resources, along with all other resources mentioned in this book, packaged as a "go-to" PDF, please visit this webpage: www.smallcapsecrets.com/resources

In this book's first chapter, we spent some time discussing terminology. I told you that any stock that sells for less than $5 a share is, technically, a penny stock. Quite a number of small caps do, in fact, fall into that category. And often, these small caps can show large returns. These stocks are usually traded as Pink Sheets or on the OTCBB.

As part of your self-education, you'll need to acquire some knowledge of the important SEC filings and how they work. I'll go into this in more detail in later. For now, I'll just give you a brief overview.

Federal securities laws require all but the smallest of companies to file reports with the SEC.

Generally speaking, any company with less than $10 million in assets doesn't have to file reports with the SEC (though many choose to). However, any company that wants to sell stocks to the public is required to either register with the SEC or qualify for an exemption. There are several kinds of exemptions, but two are quite common:

1. Regulation A
   – For companies that raise less than $5 million a year—which only requires the filing of an "offering circular" containing financial statements and other information.
2. Regulation D
   – For companies that seek to raise $1 million dollars a year, or seek $5 million but sell to 35 or fewer individuals, or for some companies with large private offerings of securities—which requires the filing of a "Form D," that contains the names and addresses of owners and stock promoters, but little else.

A public company is required to register with the SEC if it has 500 or more investors and $10 million or more in assets (this is a big reason why Facebook had to file its initial public offering), or if it is listed on one of the following stock exchanges:

- American Stock Exchange (AMEX)
- Boston Stock Exchange (BSE)
- Chicago Stock Exchange (CHX)
- Cincinnati Stock Exchange (CSE)
- NASDAQ Stock Exchange (NASDAQ)
- New York Stock Exchange (NYSE)
- Pacific Exchange
- Philadelphia Stock Exchange (PHLX)

There are two ways for a company to become public:
1. By issuing securities in an offering or transaction that is registered with the SEC.
2. By registering a company and its outstanding securities with the SEC.

Once registered, a company must file periodic reports that contain information about its business, its financial condition, and its management.

There are minimum listing standards for companies that trade their stocks on the NASDAQ, which include minimum net assets and maximum numbers of shareholders. Companies on OTCBB or Pink Sheets do not have to meet these minimum standards.

Since 2000, all companies on OTCBB have been required to file updated financial reports with the SEC. Any companies that refuse to file timely reports with the SEC or their banking and insurance regulators are removed from the OTCBB, or prevented from trading until the reports are filed. When an OTCBB company fails to file its reports on time, these companies are forced to add an "E" to their stock symbol, and the company has 30 days to file with the SEC, or 60 days to file with its banking or insurance regulator. After this grace period, it is removed from the OTCBB. Securities that have been removed from the OTCBB are listed at www.otcbb.com.

SEC filings are done electronically through the SEC'S *Electronic Data Gathering and Retrieval System* (EDGAR). You can access and download filings on public companies for free at www.sec.gov/edgar.

Now you're ready to educate yourself in the language of investing. Investment books are filled with jargon and abbreviations, so I have compiled a list to help you navigate through them.

Common Investment Abbreviations

AICPA	America Institute of Certified Public Accountants
APT	Arbitrage Pricing Theory
CAPM	Capital Asset Pricing Model
CRSP	Center for Research in Securities Prices (Chicago)
EBITDA	Earnings Before Interest, Taxes, Depreciation, & Amortization
EDGAR	Electronic Data Gathering, Analysis, & Retrieval
EMA	Exponential Moving Average
EMT	Efficient Market Theory
EPS	Earnings Per Share
EFT	Exchange-Traded Fund
FASB	Financial Accounting Standards Board
ICAPM	Inter-temporal Capital Asset Pricing Model
IPO	Initial Public Offering
GAAP	Generally Accepted Accounting Principles
MACD	Moving Average Convergence/Divergence
MPT	Modern Portfolio Theory

NRD	Narrow-Range Day
OTCBB	Over the Counter Bulletin Board
PEG	Price/Earnings to Growth Ratio
P/E RATIO	Price-to-Earnings Ratio
PSN	Plan Sponsor Network
PIPE	Private Investments in Public Equities
REIT	Real Estate Investment Trust
RSI	Relative Strength Indicator
SAI	Statement of Additional Information
SBIC	Small Business Investment Company

To download these abbreviations, along with all other abbreviations in this book, packaged as a "go-to" PDF, please visit this webpage: www.smallcapsecrets.com/abbreviations

One of the reasons investors are interested in small caps is because they've seen small companies outgrow their cap size and become corporate behemoths. Look at the stories of Dell, Microsoft, and Wal-Mart, for example.

When Dell (DELL) went public in June 1988, it was a small cap company valued at $200 million. Using the strategy of direct sales marketing, it took the world by storm, raising $30 million in its initial public offering.

Microsoft (MSFT), starting with a $488 million market cap, reached $200 billion by 2008. Wal-Mart (WMT) went public with a $21 million cap, soaring to $200 billion by 2008. These were small caps with vision.

While small caps with the right stuff can achieve such miracles—and bring windfalls to those who invest in them—it takes hard work to pick out future Dells, Microsofts, and Wal-Marts. The market for small caps may be inefficient, and individual investors may have an edge over large institutional investors, but investment miracles don't happen without instinct, knowledge, and strategy.

As with stocks, there are terminology issues pertaining to the different kinds of investors. There's the "value investor," who's looking for great prices, and the "growth investor," who's looking for companies that are slated for future profitability. In my mind, there's no point to classify yourself one way or the other. A smart investor is both.

What you need is an intelligent and systematic way to search for and identify the right small caps.

Begin by seeking out companies that are undervalued by the market. They can be new companies with innovative ideas, or companies that are not new but are turning themselves around and moving a new direction. In either case, they should be lean and hungry, with management that is efficient and accessible, and able to both promote innovation and bring it to market. The companies you're interested in should have sound policies of managerial compensation that do not interfere with the growth of the company. They should operate in sectors that are strong and viable. They should offer products and services that are in demand. They should be competitive, and have a reputation for satisfying their customers. They should have sound fundamentals and valuation, consistent working capital ratios, and good cash flow policies.

Their growth, in terms of revenues and earnings, should be at least 20% a year, with very little change in the dollar amount of expenses.

In this book, I'll go over the must-reads and must-dos that will help you choose winning small caps. I'll tell you how to study management and get an insider's perspective. I'll give you a crash course in reading financial statements and doing fundamental analysis. I'll introduce you to the basics of technical analysis. I'll give you pointers on interpreting financial guidance.

By the time you finish this book, you'll know what you need to do to assess a company and decide whether to invest in it.

At this point, though, you are at the beginning of the process. Let's keep it moving...

It's not all that hard to narrow down your search through the thousands of publicly held companies to find what you are looking for. First and foremost, you need to follow your instinct about what lies ahead. You can begin by compiling a list of small caps that you're interested in and drawn to, and ask yourself what it is about them that has peaked your interest. One way to hear about these companies is to subscribe to a few high-quality internet newsletters that issue alerts and press releases about small caps (just like we do at www.smallcapsecrets.com). At the same time, think about trends—business trends, technology trends, social trends, economic trends, and political trends. Think about what's becoming obsolete and what's taking its place. Think about the kinds of companies you think *should* be successful in the world of tomorrow.

Then comes the hard part: seeking out and learning to analyze the information you need about individual companies and their stocks.

This is a critical step in successful small cap investing. Since small caps are less studied, it's up to you to find and embrace the appropriate data. Though this sounds intimidating, it's not.

Read on.

GETTING TO KNOW SMALL CAPS

T HE HARD PART is about to begin. But, if you want to be more than just a small cap fan, you have to do some work. I wouldn't be so confident myself if I hadn't also paid my dues. So, bear with me, and try to take it all in.

Getting to know and assess a company requires a great deal of hard work and due diligence. It requires seeking out and absorbing whatever information is available.

It requires scrolling for facts and figures, talking to people, and reading. It requires analyzing everything you read in order to make the necessary interpretations, predictions, and judgments.

It requires getting to know the company's organizational plan and management, and interacting with the people who direct and manage it.

The first thing you need to do is find out basic information about a company you're considering investing in. Along with a prospectus and an annual report, you will probably receive news releases and reprints of articles and speeches made by management. (You can download most of these items from the company's website.)

Be sure, also, to take whatever additional information is available— such as newsletters, sales and marketing materials, and product information. Feel free to reach out to a company directly, if you feel you need even more information.

Reading the material you've gathered will give you a sense of the company's attitude, approach, and level of professionalism. It will also give you a good idea of the relationship it cultivates with the public.

For perspective on the company and how it is regarded, talk to industry professionals, trade associations, and even competitors. Talk to employees and former employees, if you can find them. And don't forget to speak to the company's suppliers and customers, if you can find them, too.

It's also worth checking into any legal filings mentioned in the company's publicly filed disclosure documents. True, legal documents are complicated and sometimes impossible to read, but they do contain useful and important information that you might not find elsewhere.

While it's really important that you study the company's financial statement and latest annual and quarterly reports, it's a good idea to examine its public company federal filings first.

The initial decision about whether to invest in a small cap can often be made based on these SEC filings alone. For example, any irregularities, or any conflicts of interest between the company and its management and outside directors will show up, if you read carefully. These clues, together with the financial information you've gathered (and the skills you're about to learn) will enable you to eliminate the companies you're not interested in.

Today, all public companies are required to provide "full and timely accurate public disclosure of material information." There is, however, a lot of debate about what constitutes material information. Many companies provide only what they have to in order to meet disclosure requirements.

While companies are allowed to keep some information confidential—mostly in order to protect property and technology—some companies use confidentiality to mask problems that exist within the company. It's up to you as an investor to judge this for yourself. If the management isn't willing to discuss a problem of limited information, it's generally best to move on and look elsewhere.

The most important information on any publicly held company is contained in its filings with the SEC. These filings, along with other public disclosures made by a company, can be easily downloaded at www.sec.gov

The three most important SEC filings are:
1. 10-K: The Annual Report Form.
2. 10-Q: The Quarterly Report Form.
3. 8-K: The Material Current Events Form.

Later, when you're ready to focus on the buying and selling patterns of the material insiders of the company, you'll need to read:
1. Form 3.
2. Form 4.
3. Form 5.

I'll discuss these later in the book.

For your benefit, I've put together a detailed synopsis of the forms 10-K, 10-Q, and 8-K filings. There is a wealth of information in these documents, so pay close attention.

Annual Report Form 10-K

Annual Report Form 10-K, the most important of these documents, represents the "full and fair disclosure" required by the federal government. There are two parts of this form.

Section 1 of 10-K contains a full description of the company's principal business and products or services, and the number of people it employs. It also identifies the company's principal markets and methods of distribution. Specifically:

- It details competitive factors such as patents, licenses, franchises, work backlogs, and available raw materials.
- It provides the estimate costs of research and development.
- It describes any litigation involving the company, the effects of new or pending environmental regulations, and any revenue and net income that accounted for more than 10% of sales or pretax income for the preceding five years.
- It describes the company's operations and any changes in accounting practices. It lists the locations of the company's principal facilities, together with additional capital assets, properties, or leases.
- It gives information on earnings and dividends per share for the last five years (clearly an important piece of information for an investor).
- It provides a great deal of useful information about the company's securities, including:
  a) all parent and subsidiary companies, with their respective percentage of voting securities,
  b) any increase or decrease in outstanding securities, and any reacquired or newly issued securities used in an exchange, and

   c) all holders of record for each class of equity securities, as of the end of the fiscal year.

- It lists all corporate executive officers, positions and offices held, and family relationships among such officers. It explains any policy by which any director or officer is indemnified or assured against any liability.
- It lists all financial statements prepared by the company and reviewed by the company's independent auditors.

Section 2 contains five items. (Companies sometimes substitute a proxy statement for the annual meeting, since these items are subject to periodic votes by the board of directors or the shareholders.) Those items:

- List securities owned by each of the officers and directors (and the amount and percentage of those securities by class), together with a list of any owners of 10% or more of any class of securities.
- List the names, offices, and terms of office for each director and officer, together with a description of the business and biographical background of each.
- List the directors and the three highest-paid officers, together with the aggregate fees and remuneration of all the officers and directors. (This is clearly very significant to an investor.)
- Describe options for officers and management to purchase securities from the beginning of each fiscal year, together with the vesting price of the options.
- Describe significant transactions or material changes involving assets, pension, savings or loans, and loans to officers or directors (with the business interests of those officers or directors will benefit).

Quarterly Report Form 10-Q

Quarterly Report Form 10-Q, which must be filed within 45 days of the end of each of the first three fiscal quarters, requires slightly less detail than the 10-K, and does not have to be audited by outside auditors.

Material Current Events Form 8-K

Material Current Events Form 8-K, which only needs to be filed when a key even occurs at the corporate level of the company, contains important information that may not appear anywhere else:

- Any change in control in the company.
- Any material legal proceedings against the company.
- The acquisition or disposition of assets other than those acquired or disposed in the normal course of business.
- The material substitution or withdrawal of assets that may be securing any class of registered securities such as mortgage bonds.
- Changes in securities that entail a material change to the rights of shareholders of any class of registered securities.
- Any increase of more than 5% in the amount outstanding of any class of securities.
- The default of any securities or debt obligations, not covered within 30 days, which affects more than 5% of the company's assets.
- Any decrease of more than 5% in the amount outstanding of any class of securities.
- Any options issued to purchase securities, of which the total amount exceeds 5% of the securities outstanding.
- A description of any matters submitted to a vote by shareholders.
- Any charges or credits related to unusual material events, including losses or restatements of capital or shareholder's equity account.
- Any change in the company's auditors, whether voluntary or involuntary.
- Any important event that the company considers material to its operations.

- Any changes or amendments to financial statements represented in a previously filed 10-K or 10-Q report.

Whew! You're done. Pat yourself on the back, and proceed to the next chapter at your own risk.

THE MANAGEMENT

WHEN IT COMES TO investment advice, one of the most common things you'll hear from people—investors or not—is "study the management!" Well, sure, it's good, sound advice—like "drink chicken soup if you have a cold!" But, does anyone ever tell you what they mean by studying management, or how you're supposed to go about it? No. You're left to figure that out for yourself.

"Study the management" is one of the most tired clichés in investing. It's also one of the most important things you can do. Yet, it's something that no one ever really defines.

To some, it entails a few simple steps that come before the "real" work of calculations, projections, valuations, analysis:

1. Put in a call to or email Investor Relations at a company you're researching and ask polite but incisive questions.
2. Scrutinize the résumés of top management.
3. Check out the company's organizational structure.
4. Read what analysts are saying.

But taking a robotic and uninspired approach to studying management is just plain dumb—not to mention risky. How can you really study management without meeting the people at the top, engaging them, meeting their employees, talking to their competition?

In this chapter, then, we're going to talk about *really* studying management.

As you already know, one of the great advantages of small caps is the fact that they are not widely studied by institutional investment analysts. They operate in a relatively "inefficient market," which makes it easier to beat the system in terms of the pricing of shares.

There is another real advantage of working with small caps, and that is in terms of access to management. An investor need not feel intimidated by an enormous, impersonal, indifferent institution. Small caps are eager for investors, since there are fewer shares available and there is less liquidity. The prospect of active investors taking an interest in their companies means that institutional investors will start to notice them and share prices will rise. It means that they will have an increased prospect of growth—and success.

As I'd mentioned earlier in the book, it's easy to compare the relationship between the small cap investor to that of the venture capitalist, in that the *agent*—the entrepreneur seeking out investors—is in a comparable position to the *principal* of venture capital theory—the investor who provides funds for the company.

There are, of course, significant differences:
1. Venture capital investment involves private equity, whereas the small cap is publicly held.
2. The funds in a venture capital investment go to the company, whereas they go to the selling shareholder in a small cap situation.

3. The funds available to the venture capitalist are massive, whereas those of the individual investor are comparatively modest.

It makes sense, then, for the small cap investor to use an investment strategy similar to that of the venture capitalist. The venture capitalist works with a company that's seeking funds by studying it carefully before investing, monitoring the company once the project has begun, and providing incentives for the entrepreneur to create profit. The key element in this model is that the venture capitalist takes a strong and interactive position with the management of the company.

If I learned anything from my Wall Street days, it's that an investor has the right to engage actively with the management of a small cap. This is how the big boys do it, and this is how you should too.

A small cap with big dreams requires management that is exceptional—management that has both entrepreneurial drive and corporate vision. To engage with this kind of company, you must familiarize yourself, in a real way, with upper level management. You must make it your business to get to know them, and follow what they are doing. (When you're dealing with a public company, this is not hard to do, since the information you need is publicly available.)

You need to study the *material insiders* of the company—the people who comprise its top management team. Studying what they're doing tells you a lot about the direction in which the company is heading. The buying and selling patterns of management insiders— the officers and directors of a public company—is a very significant indicator of future stock performance. And it is not hard to do, because they, like the companies themselves, are required to file documents with the SEC.

Specifically, they must file three disclosures about stock ownership: Form 3, Form 4, and Form 5. Form 3, an initial disclosure of an insider's holding of company stock, needs to be filed within 10 days of becoming an insider (even if the insider owns no shares). Any changes in stock holdings must be filed on Form 4, by the 10th day of the following months. And Form 5 must be filed by all insiders within 45 days of the end of the company's fiscal year.

The most significant insider trades are those that are sold in the open market at the current market price—without company options—since they reflect the insider's views of the future prospects of the company. Buying and selling by a cluster of company insiders after a decline in share price is particularly telling. If a group of insiders sells after a price decline, it is a bad sign; if, on the other hand, they buy after such a decline, it is a very good sign—especially if the purchases are large. It indicates that something major is about to take place.

Beyond this, you should meet several times with the key management people—to check them out, find out who the real decision makers are, and establish lines of communication. You should study their résumés, and notice things like whether they worked together or attended the same schools, or whether they were involved in selling previous companies. It's a good idea to note whether any of the key players have an investment banking background, since this might indicate plans to fix up the company and sell it. Now is the time to find out about the company's internal reporting procedures, its systems for evaluating data, its checks and balances, and its compensation structure.

Study the company's organizational chart—and that of any affiliated companies that it owns—but even more importantly—figure out for yourself whether the company really runs the way it says it does. You need to pay careful attention to the management's style—to its level of communication and collaboration. These are things that can only be determined through personal interaction and careful judgment.

Investing in small caps is largely about investing in the people who run them. The things you find out from a company's financial guidance, annual reports, financial statements, public filings, and legal documents, are only of use if you have a firm sense of belief in the people who run the company.

This sounds a bit over-the-top, doesn't it?

Well, you wouldn't buy a diamond wondering if it might be a cubic zirconia—no matter how dazzled you were by its appearance— would you? To protect yourself from being duped, you'd want to make sure you were buying it from someone reputable, right? Well, it's the same with a company that looks great on paper. It may dazzle you, but end up not being bogus. So, follow my advice— don't judge a company until you really know the people who run it.

FUNDAMENTALS

REGARDLESS OF WHETHER your life philosophy is "everything happens for a reason," or "things just happen," you still go about your business and *do* things. What's the point of sitting around doing nothing?

It's really the same with stocks. There are certain things you just do regardless of your investment philosophy. You determine a company you'd like to study—whether you get that information from a newsletter or elsewhere. You study the company and figure out how it works. You study its financials to gauge whether it's worth investing in. You do the things that can help you draw the right conclusions. You make a move.

Having said that, you need to learn the basics so you can do everything in your power—regardless of science, fate, serendipity, or the stars—to bring home winners.

When it gets down to it, you need to learn the two most important kinds of analysis: *fundamental analysis* and *technical analysis*.

(I'll warn you now... You're approaching another dull patch. So, get up and stretch, go for a jog, or have some coffee—whatever it takes to get yourself into the right frame of mind. This is stuff you need to know.)

Let's get started. There are two basic kinds of analysis that are used to examine stocks: They reflect two very different principles, and use methods that are not alike.

According to traditional investment advice:
1. *Fundamental* analysts believe that financial results are the only reliable means of establishing a company's value. They are not interested in stock charts.
2. *Technical* analysts believe that stock prices can only be determined by using charts to plot price trends. They think financial information is already out of date by the time you obtain it.

In my view, it's a waste of time arguing over which approach is better. As with everything, the more you know, the better off you are. It's as simple as that. Fundamental analysis gives you a way of interpreting the financial data of a company and technical analysis uses charts to enable you to follow stock price trends.

This chapter is about fundamental analysis. The next is about technical analysis.

Fundamental analysis uses real data—like revenues, earnings, profit margins, future growth, and return on equity—to evaluate value. Its focus is on interpreting the financial statements of a company. (By the way, reading financial statements is said to be Warren Buffet's claim to fame, so if you need the support of popular icons, you've got it.)

The accounting guidelines used by public companies are known as *generally accepted accounting principles* (GAAP). These guidelines are determined by the *American Institute of Certified Public Accountants* (AICPA) and the *Financial Accounting Standards Board* (FASB). These guidelines, though meant to promote standardization in the reporting of financial information, are somewhat flexible, and allow room for the bending of rules.

In addition, accounting standards are so complex that even accountants have trouble figuring them out. This has gotten worse, not better, since the *Sarbanes-Oxley Act*—designed to regulate accountants, executives, and security analysts in reporting to the public and disclosing potential conflicts of interest—was passed by Congress in 2002. This is another reason why it's so important to understand the basics of fundamental analysis.

Public companies use the accrual system, as opposed to non-public companies, which use cash accounting. The accrual system allows companies to record revenues and expenses in the period in which they accrue—when they come into existence. Companies use accruals for:
1. Revenue that has been earned but not yet received.
2. Revenue that has been received before it was earned.
3. Accrued expenses or costs.
4. Prepaid expenses or costs.

Accruals are useful, but they can be manipulated—for example, by listing dishonest earnings outcomes to make a company's earnings look more consistent, over time, than they really are. This can be especially true with small caps, whose growth produces more unpredictable earnings.

Let's get started learning how to analyze financial statements. (If you already know how, feel free to skip to the next chapter).

Each financial statement has three component parts:
1. A balance sheet.
2. An income statement.
3. A cash flow statement.

Balance Sheet

The balance sheet summarizes the balances of assets and liabilities. There are many things in the balance sheet that can tip you off that a company is worth—or not worth—investing in.

The balance sheet is broken down into two parts:
1. Assets: Cash, receivables, inventory, and property plant and equipment.
2. Liabilities: Current liabilities, long-term liabilities, and shareholder equity (assets minus liabilities, or net worth).

Current Assets include cash and cash equivalents, short-term investments, net receivables, inventory, and other assets. They are current because they're either cash or will be converted into cash within a year. They're listed in order of their liquidity, or how easily they can be converted into cash.

All other assets are listed immediately below *Current Assets*. They consist of property plant and equipment, intangible assets, long-term investments, goodwill, accumulated amortization, other assets, and deferred long-term asset charges. *Long-term assets* include building, vehicles, machinery, and equipment, and the net value of depreciation written off as expenses in a year.

Current Liabilities include money that is owed within the year, including cash and short-term investments, total inventory, total receivables, and prepaid expenses. *Long-term Liabilities* are those due in one year or more; they include bank loans, bond loans, unpaid taxes, and money owed to vendors.

Current assets—also referred to as "working assets"—fuel the entire cycle of cash in the company. Cash is used to buy inventory; inventory is sold to vendors, and becomes cash receivable; accounts receivable turn it back into cash. This cycle is how the company makes money. It's clearly a pretty important factor in investment decisions.

High amounts of cash (and cash equivalents) are usually, but not always, a good thing. If the company is generating a lot of money because it has a competitive advantage—this is a great indicator. If, however, tons of cash comes from selling either a business or a large number of bonds, it may not be so good.

The easiest way to find this out is to go through past balance sheets and see if there's been a high level of debt and/or sales of new shares or assets. If not, and the company is generating cash, it's probably a good bet, because cash is crucial to getting through the hard times any company is likely to experience.

There are three important ratios that can be gleaned from the balance sheet:
1. Current ratio.
2. Quick assets ratio.
3. Debt ratio.

The *current ratio* equals the sum of current assets divided by the sum of current liabilities. *As a general rule, this ratio should be two or higher*; if it is, there's a reasonable chance that there will be enough cash to pay current bills and future obligations.

(There are, however, some companies with a durable competitive advantage with current ratios below one. In such companies, strong earning power makes it possible to early cover current liabilities. The key here is consistency of earnings.)

What's in a Balance Sheet?
($ in millions)

Assets	Liabilities
Cash & Short-term Investments	Accounts Payable
Total Inventory	Accrued Expenses
Total Receivables, Net	Short-Term Debt
Prepaid Expenses	Long-Term Debt
Other Current Assets, Total	Other Current Liabilities
Total current Assets	Total Current Liabilities
Property/Plant/Equipment	Long-Term Debt
Goodwill, Net	Deferred Income Tax
Intangibles, Net	Minority Interest
Long-Term Investments	
Other Long-Term Assets	Other Liabilities
	Total Liabilities
Other Assets	
Total Assets	

Shareholder's Equity
Preferred Stock
Common Stock
Additional Paid in Capital
Retained Earnings
Treasury Stock—Common

Other Equity
Total Shareholder's Equity
Total Liabilities & Shareholder's Equity

Sample Balance Sheet

Business Name
Business Address
Suburb

Balance Sheet
As of 31 December 2009

Assets

Current Assets

Cash On Hand	$100.00	
Cash at Bank	$4,706.07	
Trade Debtors	$32,532.00	
Total Current Assets		$37,338.07

Non-Current Assets

Shares in listed companies	$75,000.00	
Loan - Associated Entities	$5,000.00	
Office Equipment	$3,500.00	
Total Non-Current Assets		$83,500.00

Total Assets		$120,838.07

Liabilities

Current Liabilities

Trade Creditors	$25,130.00	
Other Creditors	$3,000.00	
Provision for Tax	$1,525.00	
Total Current Liabilities		$29,655.00

Non-Current Liabilities

Bank Loans	$50,000.00	
Hire Purchase	$14,095.00	
Total Non-Current Liabilities		$64,095.00

Total Liabilities		$93,750.00

Net Assets		$27,088.07

Equity

Investor A

Investor A - Capital	$65,000.00	
Investor A - Drawings	($62,206.73)	
Total Investor A		$2,793.27

Investor B

Investor B - Capital	$65,000.00	
Investor B - Drawings	($42,300.00)	
Total Investor B		$22,700.00

Total Investors' Equity		$25,493.27
Current Year Profit / (Loss)		$1,594.80
Total Equity		$27,088.07

To download these tables, along with all other tables in this book, packaged as a "go-to" PDF, please visit this webpage: www.smallcapsecrets.com/tables

If a company has a large inventory, the *quick assets ratio* is used in place of the current ratio. The quick assets ratio is a better indicator of true working capital in a company that has high inventory levels throughout the year. This ratio is calculated the same way as the current ratio, except it excludes the asset value of its inventory. *The ideal standard for this ratio is one or higher.*

And, finally, there is the *debt ratio*, which equals the long-term debt balance divided by the total capitalization. The debt ratio indicates how much of the company's capitalization is comprised of debt.

This is an important indicator of the likely success or failure of the company as an investment. Look out for a percentage of debt that is growing over time; that is a definite red flag. *What you want to see is a debt ratio that is either very steady or falling over a span of years.* After all, you don't want to invest in a company that will be spending its future earnings on debt plus interest instead of investing in growth and/or paying dividends.

Income Statement

The income statement is the most important part of a company's financial statement. It shows the net profit or loss incurred over a specific period—either a fiscal quarter or a year (as compared to the balance sheet, which represents a single moment in time).

52

The income statement is divided into two parts—operating and non-operating expenses. The first section is especially important from an investment point of view, as it provides information about revenues and expenses that result directly from the regular business operations of a company. The second section discloses revenue and expense information about activities that aren't directly related to the company's regular operations—for example, the selling of plant equipment.

The three most important items on the income statement are:
1. Gross profit.
2. Net operating profit.
3. Earnings per share.

Gross profit is the net difference between revenues and the cost of goods sold—in other words, profit before operating expenses have been deducted. The gross profit margin indicates whether the relationship between revenue and costs remains stable as revenues expand.

Net operating profit equals revenues minus costs and expenses. It does not include any profit earned from the company's investments, or the effects of interest and taxes.

Net profit is further adjusted for non-operating income and expenses and for tax liabilities—resulting in *earnings per share* (EPS).

The income statement also indicates the number of shares of stock issued and outstanding, which in turn can be used to calculate market capitalization. (Clearly, for an investor seeking out small caps, knowing where to find this is important.)

What's in an Income Statement?

($ in millions)

Operating Expenses
Selling, General & Administrative
Research & Development

Depreciation
Operating Profit
Interest Expense
Gain (Loss) Sale Assets

Other
Income before Tax

Income Taxes Paid
Net Earnings

To download these tables, along with all other tables in this book, packaged as a "go-to" PDF, please visit this webpage: www.smallcapsecrets.com/tables

(Sample Income Statement included on the next page.)

Sample Income Statement

Income Statement
For the Three Months Ending March 31, 2006

		Year to Date	
Revenues			
Landscaping Fees	$	20,075.00	99.50
Finance Charge Income		100.00	0.50
Total Revenues		20,175.00	100.00
Cost of Sales			
Total Cost of Sales		0.00	0.00
Gross Profit		20,175.00	100.00
Expenses			
Auto Expense		2,200.00	10.90
Commissions and Fees Exp		6,000.00	29.74
Dues and Subscriptions Exp		600.00	2.97
Insurance Expense		250.00	1.24
Total Expenses		9,050.00	44.86
Net Income	$	11,125.00	55.14

To download these tables, along with all other tables in this book, packaged as a "go-to" PDF, please visit this webpage: www.smallcapsecrets.com/tables

TECHNICAL ASSESSMENT

'M GOING TO START this chapter by presenting some playful stereotypes...

On one side, we have the *Fundamentalists*—accounting types who pore over financial statements, quasi-venture capitalists who ponder corporate governance, and ordinary *schlemeils* who think you need to know about a company to gauge the worth of its stock.

On the other side, we have the *Technophiles*—computer geeks who sit at the computer all day poring over charts, fast-talking day traders scrutinizing crossovers and candlesticks, and ordinary *schlemiels* who think that all you need to do is predict trends to play the stock market.

Well, of course this is all nonsense! And so, basically, is the idea that there are two completely separate camps among investors— the ones who follow companies and the ones who follow trends. Anyone who studies the stock market knows that you have to do both.

So, without further ado, let's go to the next branch of investment: Technical Analysis.

Technical analysis is the study of the way market prices move in relation to trend. Technical analysts look at the history of a security's trading pattern, using charts and technical indicators to predict its movement. There has always been a great deal of debate about whether prediction of stock movements is valid (or even possible), but that's a moot point. The fact is that technical analysis provides useful ways of analyzing stock price and performance, and is therefore helpful for both identifying trading opportunities and timing sales.

By the way, technical analysis is no sweat today, since everything you can possibly need is on the Internet. You can enjoy the benefits of technically precise information without being bothered with the dullness of number crunching or draftsmanship. Today, you don't even have to worry about monitoring stock prices and volume, or calculating moving averages. Everything is there and waiting for you. All you need to do is figure out how to use this information. Believe me, it's not hard. (Just visit www.stockcharts.com, and take one of their free Chart School tutorials.)

Let's start with the basic concepts and terminology of technical analysis. Then I'll introduce you to the various charts and technical patterns, and show you how you can use technical indicators in your search for the right small caps.

The *trading range*, or *channel*, is the spread between the high and low prices of a stock as it's traded during a given period of time. On a chart, the trading range is the space between *resistance*, the upper price limit, and *support*, the lower price limit. Resistance—at the top of the chart—is the highest price at which a stock has sold, and support—at the bottom—is the lowest.

These three things—trading range, resistance, and support—are the most basic components of technical analysis.

A trading range that remains level across time is a *stationary trading range*; one that evolves and changes direction is a *moving trading range*. (Pretty intuitive for something so "technical," right?)

The *breadth* of the trading range—or the distance between its upper and lower limits—is an important indicator of a stock's volatility. Whether the price is moving upwards towards resistance or downwards towards support, as long as the breadth remains constant, the volatility or market risk does not change.

However, when there's a *breakdown* (Don't get nervous, now!), meaning that the price has gone above resistance or below support, the breadth itself changes, and volatility increases.

There are two basic types of pattern configurations: *continuation* and *reversal*. A continuation pattern signifies that a price will continue moving in the same direction. A reversal pattern signals a slowing down or a movement in the opposite direction.

Now comes the fun part: the chart patterns. There are several simple chart patterns that have useful interpretive value. Though it's not the easiest thing in the world to figure out how they work, the patterns themselves correspond to the first shapes you ever learned to draw:

- Triangles
  - A triangle can be a *continuation* pattern or a *reversal* pattern. There are three kinds of triangle patterns: *ascending*, *descending*, and *symmetrical*.
    i. An ascending triangle, where the point of the triangle hits the top, is considered a bullish sign.
    ii. A descending triangle, where the point of the triangle hits the bottom, is a bearish sign.
    iii. A symmetrical triangle indicates a period of consolidation where the outcome is uncertain.

- Flags and Pennants
  - Like triangles, flags and pennants are created by changes in the breadth of the trading range. They are both continuation patterns, signifying price consolidation.
  - The flag is rectangular in shape, and the pennant is triangular. The flag indicates a significant price change followed by a sideways movement. It usually ends in a price breakout—above resistance or below support. The initial spike is called the flag pole, and the horizontal trend is called the flag.
  - The main difference between flags and pennants is the trading range. In the flag, the breadth of the range remains the same; in the pennant, it changes.
- Double tops or double bottoms
  - In a double top, the price hits resistance twice; similarly, in a double bottom, the price hits support twice. In other words, the price spikes, retreats, then spikes again.
  - When a double top spikes without breaking through resistance, it is a sign that prices will decline. Similarly, when a double bottom spikes without breaking through support, it's a sign that prices will rise.
- Wedges
  - Similar to triangles, but they take much longer to develop (sometimes as long as several months). They contain within them at least two tests of both resistance and support—i.e. double tops and double bottoms. A falling wedge is a bullish sign, whereas a rising one is bearish.
- Head and shoulders
  - Three spikes. The middle spike, or *head*, is higher than the other two, the *shoulders*. Following a head and shoulders, prices tend to fall. Similarly, after a reverse head and shoulders, prices should rise.

- Gaps
  - Spaces found between one period's closing price and the next period's opening price. A common gap is not significant, but a *runaway gap*, a *breakaway gap*, or an *exhaustion gap* is:
    i. A runaway gap (a scary thought!) is a series of gaps, occurring in the same direction.
    ii. A breakaway gap is one that moves through resistance or support; it usually initiates a major price movement.
    iii. An exhaustion gap follows the breakaway gap, generally signaling that prices are going to change directions.
    iv. The convergence of these three trends is generally looked upon by day traders and swing traders as an *entry* or *exit signal.*

An Ascending Triangle

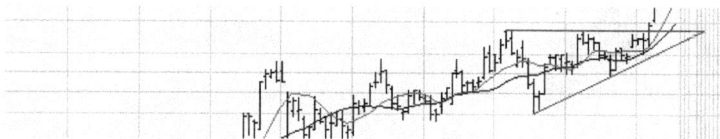

Descending Triangles

A Symmetrical Triangle

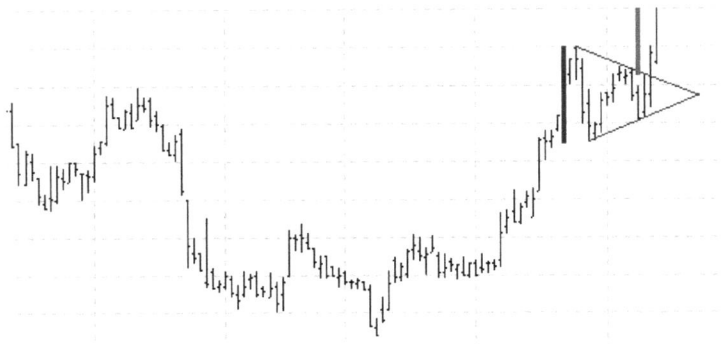

Bull Flag in an Upward Trend

A Double Top

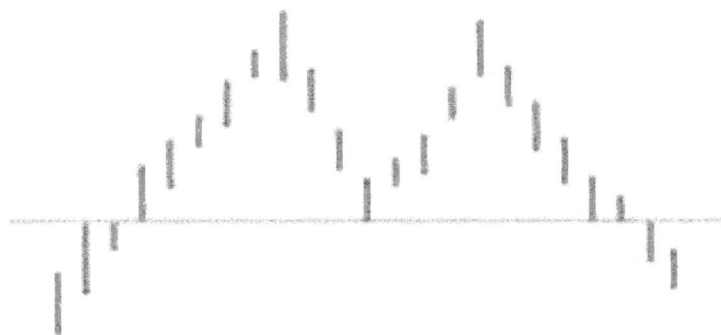

A Falling Wedge in an Upward Trend

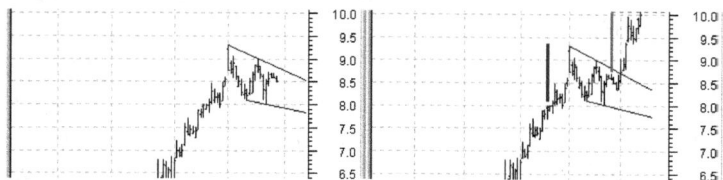

Head and Shoulders As a Reversal Pattern in an Upward Trend

To download these charts, along with all other charts in this book, packaged as a "go-to" PDF, please visit this webpage: www.smallcapsecrets.com/charts

There are two other pairs of concepts that are central to technical analysis. One is the idea of *accumulation* (buying) and *distribution* (selling), and the other is that of *convergence* and *divergence*.

It is possible to spot emerging trends in the supply and demand for shares by using an *Accumulation and Distribution* (A/D) formula:

A/D = ((Close – Low) – (High – Close)) / (Close – Low) * Volume

Similarly, convergence towards or divergence away from the current moving average of prices can be used to gauge the strength or weakness of a trend.

Moving average convergence/divergence (MACD) is considered a dynamic indicator because it applies two moving averages to current price. Using MACD, it is possible to identify three kinds of signals in stock prices: *crossover points, overbought or oversold conditions,* and *divergences.*
Finally, there is another indicator called *relative price* that is used to compare price trends in relation to other stocks within the same industry or in the larger market. The formula for calculating relative price strength is rather simple: current price divided by the index. A drop in relative price strength is a significant momentum indicator, and can be used to signal an exit.

Technical indicators are by no means foolproof, but when combined with fundamental research and analysis, they are helpful tools for timing entry and exit strategies.

Frankly speaking, I don't understand all the fuss about the word "technical analysis," since charting is rather fun if you don't have to draw the charts yourself. Charting stocks is still technical, yes. But now, with the Internet, it's positively user-friendly!

In fact, some chartists now call themselves "visual analysts." Why not?

The tantalizing digital images of stock patterns are so intriguing that they might even bring the battle between Fundamentalists and Technophiles to a halt. (I suspect there may be a growing number of diehard fundamental analysts out there who secretly check out the stock charts when no one's looking!)

SMART PREDICTIONS

S UCCESSFUL INVESTING is an odd combination of magic and brains. You have to believe in magic to think big enough to invest. But you have to really push that brain in order to turn magic into profits.

Nowhere is this truer than in the realm of financial projection. You need to "foresee"—like an ancient soothsayer following the signs of birds. But you need to do much more than follow birds to predict the future growth of a company. You need to marshal all the knowledge you've acquired about a company's management, organizational structure, documents, and financial statements to make sound predictions. And that is a tall order.

Before you start working on this task, it's important to find out what the company itself predicts about its future earnings. You can find all the information you need, including projections and valuations, in the company's *financial guidance*—its own estimate of projected earnings. Public companies issue guidance—often by way of conference calls or webcasts—just before their quarterly results are released. Some companies will update their guidance during the quarter, through press releases, or they will actually post it on their company websites.

Financial guidance is largely used to direct analysts' earnings forecasts toward what the company considers achievable, and to provide information to shareholders and potential investors. The SEC's *Fair Disclosure* rule (FD), enacted in 2000, requires that such guidance be provided to the investing community as a whole, and not just to a select group—which means that it's not just for analysts anymore.

A company's purposes in providing earnings guidance are many:
1. To underplay analyst expectations, and prevent negative surprises.
2. To reduce share price unpredictability when actual results are announced.
3. To shift the focus of investors from short-term to long-term results.

Guidance typically includes such key metrics as revenues, net income, and *earnings per share* (EPS), *earnings before interest, taxes, depreciation, and amortization* (EBITDA), and cash flow. Based on the company's own internal projections and budget, guidance provides an estimate of expected results.

Companies are, naturally, not always accurate in assessing their own growth. One of the most common errors they make is to assume that the current rate of growth will continue into the future, instead of adjusting their estimates to include the slowdown that inevitably occurs over time. Another is to base their figures of market share on known competition, without recognizing the competitive threat of smaller, less well-known companies. Sometimes, they simply take too positive or negative a view of their futures.

It's important to be able to evaluate the reliability of a company's financial guidance. As with all else, getting to know a company's management is the best way to discern whether its projections can be trusted to be objective and accurate.

Of course, not all of the predictions made about a company's future behavior are made by the company itself. Many are them are made by analysts (who sometimes incorporate the company's projections into their own forecasts without questioning their accuracy). Not surprisingly, the projections and valuations made by analysts are often taken more seriously than those made by the company itself.

This is significant for small caps, which are less studied by analysts. For many small caps, analysts are primarily junior analysts who are not as well-trained, so the chance of inaccurate predictions is even greater.

Ultimately, it's your job to sift through what you hear from the company, analysts, or newsletters. This includes being aware of the games companies can play in the act of communicating about their earnings. The most serious one is when a company manipulates its data to make it appear to meet or exceed guidance, or to conform to analyst expectations. Another is to send out press releases saying they've met their earnings estimates when they haven't.

There are several signs that can indicate that a company's books are being manipulated. These can include: earnings adjustments each year, adjustments each period for previously reported outcomes, high volatility, fluctuations in P/E and EPS, and increases in the debt ratio from year to year.

While financial guidance is extremely helpful, the predictions you make yourself are the ones that will matter the most. To do the best possible job on this, you should follow the following trends:
1. The *price earnings ratio.*
2. The *price earnings to growth.*
3. The rate of growth.
4. The *price-to-book ratio.*
5. The *price-to-free-cash-flow ratio.*

6. The company's rate of growth.

You also need to assess management's policy on executive compensation, to make sure it is not working against the company's continued growth.

The *P/E ratio* (share price divided by earnings per share) is an important metric. The kind of stocks you're looking for—those with substantial profit margins and rapid growth—most often have high P/E ratios. But there are also cases where companies with good growth prospects and outstanding business performance are trading at low P/E multiples; these, too, are excellent investments.

P/E to Growth (PEG) calculates the P/E ratio of a stock as compared to its growth rate. It is simply the P/E ratio divided by the growth rate. The PEG ratio can be calculated historically, using the previous year's number, *a trailing 12-month period*, or into the future, using guidance estimates. A lower PEG ratio is good, as it indicates promising growth at a reasonable price. A PEG ratio of one is considered optimal.

The company's rate of growth is extremely important. Generally speaking, a growth rate over 20 percent is considered positive, provided the valuation is accurate.

An important ratio that is often ignored by analysts and investors alike is the price-to-book ratio. Screening for a low price-to-book ratio (1.5 to 1) can be fruitful, as there are many financially healthy companies that trade at a market price below book value. Most often, these companies are in industries that are mundane or outside of the main stream—not development-stage industries on the cutting edge of technology, with high levels of intangible intellectual property.

The price-to-free-cash-flow-ratio, which equals market capitalization divided by free cash flow, is another useful metric. The combination of a low price-to-book figure and a low price-to-free cash flow valuation augurs well for investment success.

Small caps that trade at low price-to-book ratios, low multiples of free cash flow, or low trailing price-to earnings ratios are the ones that are most likely to outperform themselves in later periods.

Whatever the case, the right valuations and ratios, when combined with positive insider activity and high quality management, are good omens. They may not be the bird signs that an ancient seer would decipher, but they are harbingers of success nonetheless—to investors with a ready sixth sense.

HOW TO TAKE THE PLUNGE

S O, WHAT'S THE BEST WAY to take the plunge, now that you've decided to take it? Do you leave the whole business in the hands of a broker? Do you use stock options? Do you work with a small cap or micro cap fund? Do you choose an exchange-traded fund (ETF)?

Whichever way you go, you must confront the issue of low liquidity and volatility—and make sure that, when you buy or sell small caps, you are protecting yourself against loss. You also need to consider the full range of risks associated with your purchase, including those pertaining to cash flow, diversification, and taxes. And, finally, you need to make sure that your purchase works in concert with the rest of your investment portfolio, and that you are sufficiently—but not excessively—diversified.

No matter what venue you use for purchasing your small cap stocks, you should begin by familiarizing yourself with the various types of orders that can be used for making trades. Knowing what they are and how to use them gives you the power to exercise control over the price points of your trades.

There are nine basic order types available for making a stock trade:

1. A market order.
2. A limit order.
3. A stop-loss.
4. A trailing stop.
5. An all-or-none.
6. An at-or-better.
7. A good-till-canceled.
8. An on-open or on-close.
9. A day order.

A *market order* is an order to purchase a stock at the current market price. This essentially means that you are authorizing your broker to transact your order at the price prevailing at the moment of the trade. Given the high volatility of small cap stocks, a market order is not usually the most advantageous type of order. It's the one you would use if you felt the need to buy or sell a stock immediately.

A *limit order* is an order for which you specify an exact price at which the stock can be bought or sold. This is usually a safe order to use with small caps, since it allows you to control the price.

A *stop-loss* order is an order that generates a *sell* if the stock falls to a specified price level. It is used to limit potential losses and protect your downside exposure. The key is to use this type of order only if you're comfortable selling the stock at the agreed-upon price (or lower, in a fast-moving market).

A *trailing stop* is like a stop loss order, but instead of limiting losses, it protects paper profits. With this type of order, a *sell* is generated when a fixed percentage of the current market price is reached. This type of order can be somewhat risky for a small cap stock that rises quickly and retreats, since it is automatically sold, and you may not want it to be.

An *all-or-none* is an order that is used primarily by advanced traders. It's used in combination orders involving stock and option positions, and stipulates that all of the specified positions must be executed simultaneously.

An *at-or-better* order is a variation of the limit order, in which a buy or sell order is executed at or above the agreed-upon limit price.

A *good-till-cancelled* order is an order that remains open until it's either executed or canceled. This kind of order will keep your order on the books unless you change your mind and cancel it.

A *day order* is an order that is placed today and will either be executed during the current trading session or will expire. All orders except *good-till-cancelled* orders are automatically *day orders*.

An *on-open order* or an *on-close order* is an order that's executed at a specified time in the trading session—at the beginning or close of the day, respectively. This type of order is most often used by day traders.

The wide range of order types provides great flexibility in the ordering of trades—and useful protection, if you choose wisely. Determining the type of order, however, is only one part of the process; the other is recognizing and acting upon timing trends to maximize your profitability. It's vitally important to establish profit goals and bail-out points.

A *stock option* is the right to buy or sell shares of a stock at a guaranteed price for a specified period of time. There are two types: the *call*, which gives the holder the right to buy the stock at the agreed-upon price, and the *put*, which gives the holder the right to sell it. In either case, the buyer pays the seller a premium.

Options can be used on individual stocks, or on an ETF or index. Before you use them, however, it's important to figure out how they work, and to master the sometimes-confusing jargon. It's a good idea to download explanatory information from the website of the major American options exchange, the *Chicago Board Options Exchange* (CBOE), or to use its free paper trading service to learn the ropes.

As you know, you can't expect buy/sell orders or stock options to completely protect you from loss, especially in the more volatile arena of small caps. You have to do whatever you can to time your transactions intelligently.

Pay attention to any sudden spikes in volume, which indicate major occurrences—or surprising earnings announcements, which indicate revised corporate guidance or analysis. Keep abreast of changes in the trading range of the stock; if you're doing your technical analysis, look for breakthroughs in resistance or support, or triangles that indicate narrowing or broadening of the range. And, of course, watch out for any significant fundamentals, like changes in management.

One thing you can do to control the cost of buying stocks is to use *averaging* techniques: dollar cost averaging or value cost averaging. *Dollar cost averaging* involves investing in one company at regular intervals. V*alue cost averaging* involves adjusting the dollar value of a monthly share purchase, based on the performance of the stock; this technique enables you to buy more shares when the price declines, and fewer when it increases.

If you choose to purchase individual stocks, you need to decide whether to use a broker or buy your stocks directly. If you use a broker, you have a choice:
1. A full-service broker.
2. A discount broker.

3. An online broker.

If you choose a full-service broker, you will probably pay a higher commission than if you use a discount broker. The commission can usually be negotiated, but there are several other costs. Your broker makes more money from capturing the *spread* (the difference between your *bid* price and *asked* prices. The broker is also a dealer, and if you're buying OTC stocks, and may charge a *markup*.

A discount broker will charge a lower commission if you're willing to forego research reports and other full-service perks (which is fine, since you're unlikely to find anything exceptional in the way of reports for a small cap stock, anyway). A discount broker may even offer you a zero commission. But beware; the transaction might be free, but it's at the *asking price*. In some transactions, you're actually better off using a full-service broker, since—despite the higher commission—your order will be filled at *the midpoint between the bid and the asked price*. This can make a sizable difference.

If you're not concerned about getting research (remember the inefficiency of the small cap world?), you might want to use an online broker, whose commission can be less than 10% of a traditional broker's.

Banks and insurance companies are getting in on the act; some offer brokerage services along with their financial products. Sometimes you can get good deals by going this route.

For direct purchases, you can buy directly from the issuer by using a *dividend reinvestment program* (DRIP), and reinvest your cash dividends to buy more stock without using a broker. Some charge no fees and sell *no-load stocks*, but expect some administrative fees.

Now, let's move on to the question of funds and ETF's. Mutual funds are invaluable when it comes to the general management of an investment portfolio. But small caps pose a unique challenge. Large mutual funds need to buy large numbers of stocks to utilize their ample cash base, and they can't take a controlling position in any individual company. Yet small caps have limited numbers of shares to sell. Because of this, you are much more likely to have success with a smaller mutual fund that focuses exclusively on small cap stocks.

To choose the right fund, you need to evaluate the fund's stated objectives in terms of growth and value, income, level of conservatism, and risk profile. You need to make sure that it handles the kinds of stocks and bonds you want in your portfolio. You need to scrutinize the track record of the fund and its management. You need to choose a small enough fund, or even a close-end fund that will not accept new shares after a specific portfolio size has been reached). And, of course, you need to assess its fee structure.

Mutual funds vary greatly in the fees that they charge for their services. Funds that charge a *sales load* either take a large percentage fee right off the top, or charge a *deferred sales load* that is deducted from your proceeds. Load fees are generally considerable. Given that there are many no-load funds that perform equally well, I advise against them.

At the same time, all mutual funds charge various types of fees, including expenses, special charges, annual marketing or distribution fees, and "special charges." Scrutinize these carefully. I recommend using the SEC's free calculator of mutual fund fees, which can be accessed on the SEC website (www.sec.gov) under "investment tools."

For information on the mutual fund industry, Morningstar (www.morningstar.com) provides free information on comparative performance, expense ratios, fund volatility, and Morningstar's ratings.

Yahoo posts lists of the best performing small cap mutual funds, classified according to *value* and *growth*, or a blend thereof. On the following pages you'll see the five-year top performers as of February, 2012.

Top Performers - 5 Year (out of 255)
(Value)

Fund Name	Symbol	Ann. Ret.
Oceanstone Fund	OSFDX	41.49%
Intrepid Small Cap Instl	ICMZX	11.96%
Intrepid Small Cap	ICMAX	11.83%
SouthernSun Small Cap Instl	SSSIX	9.98%
SouthernSun Small Cap Investor	SSSFX	9.81%
Invesco Special Value Y	SVFDX	8.83%
Invesco US Small Cap Value Y	MPSCX	8.73%
Invesco Special Value A	SVFAX	8.55%
Invesco US Small Cap Value A	MCVAX	8.45%
Invesco Special Value B	SVFBX	7.74%

Top Performers - 5 Year (out of 569)
(Growth)

Fund Name	Symbol	Ann. Ret.
Brown Capital Mgmt Small Co Instl	BCSSX	9.59%
Brown Capital Mgmt Small Co Inv	BCSIX	9.58%
Janus Triton I	JSMGX	9.35%
Janus Triton D	JANIX	9.24%
Janus Triton T	JATTX	9.19%
Janus Triton A	JGMAX	9.02%

Fund Name	Symbol	Ann. Ret.
Janus Triton S	JGMIX	8.92%
Wells Fargo Adv Small Cap Growth I	WFSIX	8.70%
Janus Triton R	JGMRX	8.65%
Lord Abbett Developing Growth I	LADYX	8.63%

Top Performers - 5 Year (out of 484)

(Blend: Value & Growth)

Fund Name	Symbol	Ann. Ret.
Fidelity Small Cap Discovery	FSCRX	8.93%
Transamerica Small/Mid Cap Value I2	TSMVX	8.55%
PIMCO Small Cap StocksPLUS TR Inst	PSCSX	8.23%
Transamerica Small/Mid Cap Value I	TSVIX	8.21%
PIMCO Small Cap StocksPLUS TR P	PCKPX	8.06%
Transamerica Small/Mid Cap Value A	IIVAX	7.93%
PIMCO Small Cap StocksPLUS TR A	PCKAX	7.89%
PIMCO Small Cap StocksPLUS TR D	PCKDX	7.84%
Dreyfus Opportunistic Small Cap	DSCVX	7.83%
TFS Small Cap	TFSSX	7.79%

To download these tables, along with all other tables in this book, packaged as a "go-to" PDF, please visit this webpage: www.smallcapsecrets.com/tables

The *exchange-traded fund* (ETF), a newer kind of investment fund, has become a highly viable and increasingly popular alternative to the mutual fund. Because the investments of an ETF are predefined, its fees are lower. Also, since ETFs trade on a stock exchange, they can be traded whenever the exchange is open.

Whatever way you choose to purchase your small cap stocks, and however you choose to diversify and allocate your investment portfolio, there are limitless strategies on purchasing small and micro cap stocks.

This is one area where the most dynamic investor needs to slow down and think. Paying close attention to the details of buying and selling is one of the best ways to protect your investment—and reward yourself for being gutsy enough—and brilliant enough— to invest in small caps!

ALLOCATION, ALLOCATION, ALLOCATION

DON'T ADVOCATE you rushing out and putting all your money into small caps. You're my *protégé*, after all! I want to see you set things up properly, so you can enjoy playing with your small caps without living on the edge.

Think back to the questions I asked you about your personal risk level. Think back to the investment goals I asked you to write down.

Now let's take these two things—personal risk level and investment goals—and place them into a practical context. How do you envision small caps fitting into your investment life? How do you want them to fit into your investment portfolio?

Whatever you decide, you need to make sure you diversify your portfolio. Not diversifying is dangerous for anyone. A small cap investor has to be smart, and can't afford to be haphazard.

Small caps are equities. Equities comprise one asset class, but any good portfolio should have two other components: fixed income and alternatives. Fixed income consists of bonds and bond funds. Bonds are less volatile than stocks, so they're especially important if you want to focus on small caps. Alternatives include real estate and hard assets such as commodities.

Now you need to figure out an allocation that makes sense, feels comfortable, and accommodates your new avocation—small cap investing.

Here are a few sample portfolio allocation ranges:
1. If you're young, healthy, successful, and willing to handle a high level of risk:
   - Fixed income   1%-15%
   - Equities   60%-80%
   - Alternatives   15%-35%
2. If you're older, have family obligations, and prefer less risk:
   - Fixed income   15%-35%
   - Equities   40%-60%
   - Alternatives   15%-35%

As a small cap aficionado, you need to go a step further, and establish what percentage of your equities is going to be comprised of small caps. This decision should be based on the same factors as your financial goals, but also on the correlation between small caps and other assets.

The kind of correlation you're looking for is *negative correlation*: you want the various elements of your portfolio to work differently, but in conjunction with each other, so they produce overall stability. Without stability in your portfolio, the excitement of small cap investing will turn into frenzy.

Diversification doesn't stop here. It's not just your overall investment portfolio that needs diversifying. Your small caps need balance and complementarity, too.

The way to achieve this balance depends very much on how you choose to buy your stocks—individually, through a small cap mutual fund, or an ETF, or through a combination of the three. If you go for a mutual fund or ETF, the way your small cap portfolio is diversified will depend largely on the particular fund or ETF you purchase.

To make this decision, you need to realistically assess:
1. How much time you have—and want—to put into finding and researching small caps.
2. How experienced you are in investing.
3. How confident you are about going it alone.
4. How much control you want over your small cap portfolio.
5. How closely you want to be involved in the companies you invest in.

If you choose to buy individual stocks, the best way to achieve a diversified portfolio is to:
1. Invest in 5-15 small caps—enough to protect against the possibility of bad luck or poor choices, but not enough to create a huge organizational burden for yourself, and…
2. Choose companies from different sectors and market segments, to ensure that they're not all subject to the same external events or factors.

If you choose to purchase a mutual fund or ETF, diversification will be built in. If you go with a small cap mutual fund, which typically includes 50-200 individual stocks, or a small cap ETF such as the iShares Russell 2000, which handles 2,000 individual stocks, you do not need to be as daring or vigilant as you would be if purchasing stocks individually.

If you choose to do all three, you can achieve optimal diversification by purchasing 3 or 4 individual small caps, a small cap mutual fund, and an ETF.

Whatever you do, however, be sure to periodically rebalance your small cap portfolio as well as your total portfolio. Don't forget, the whole point of choosing small caps wisely is to discover some that will quickly grow into large caps. Once they do so, your correlations will change, and you need to reestablish a new mix to ensure the right balance of returns.

Well, you've just finished the penultimate chapter. Put a feather in your cap!

FINAL THOUGHTS

YOU KNOW WHAT IT'S LIKE when you go house-hunting? A good imagination enables you to see through *kitsch* and chaos and bad decorating. It gives you the power to see what's underneath—great space, great lines, and great potential. It gives you permission to take a risk.

With this kind of power, you can pick a winner and buy it for a song. Then, with a little effort and hard work—and money, of course—you can transform that bargain into dream house.

Well, that's what it's all about with small cap trading.

You let your imagination, brains, and common sense lead you to companies that are special. You don't have to care about the externals—the fake grandiosity of the ordinary and the safe. You go for the inner greatness, the potential. Then you take a leap!

If you take this approach, you'll find companies that deserve to be discovered. You'll find entrepreneurs who want you to invest in their companies. You'll find not only wealth but satisfaction.

To me, great entrepreneurs are visionaries—like great artists, philosophers, or scientists.

And so are great small cap investors. They're not in it just for the money. They see the future coming and choose to invest in it.

So, this is the personal secret that I bequeath to you: *Trusting yourself to take risks is what makes small cap investing work.*

And now, without the crutch of financial rhetoric, let me share with you some small cap success stories.

I briefly touched upon the small cap successes of Microsoft, Dell, and Wal-Mart. These are the companies that everyone knows about—the champions of technology.

But there are success stories all around you—in every sector, not just technology.

All but one of the ten best performing stocks of the past decade in the Russell 3000 Index started out as a small cap. The nine small cap companies on the list represent a wide range of industries—sodas and sports drinks, outdoor footwear, restaurant equipment, healthcare information software, and mining—as well technology.

And at the same time, six of the ten best-performing stocks of the last three years are *still* small caps:

- Pier 1 Imports, a retailer of decorative accessories, furniture, and housewares, with a market value of $1.9 billion.
- Keryx Biopharmaceuticals, a developer of products for the treatment of diabetes and cancer, with a market value of $299 million.
- Select Comfort, a manufacturer of air beds, with a market value of $1.8 billion.

- Mitek Systems, a developer of software used for document processing and forgery detection, with a market value of $302 million.
- Pharmacyclics, a developer of pharmaceuticals used to treat certain cancers and cardiovascular disease, with a market value of $1.8 billion.

It takes people who have not only studied the rudiments of investing, but are also ingenious, gutsy, imaginative thinkers—to discover such companies, and choose to invest in them.

If you think you are one of those, then go for it!

Small cap investing is the most exciting thing in the world—if you're not afraid to think big and play your hand.

So go, have a great time, and make yourself a fortune!

GLOSSARY[1]

AMERICAN
DEPOSITARY
RECEIPT
(ADR)

A negotiable security that represents securities of a non-US company that trade in the US financial markets. Securities of a foreign company that are represented by an ADR are called American Depositary Shares (ADRs).

Shares of many non-US companies trade on US stock exchanges through ADRs. ADRs are denominated and pay dividends in US dollars and may be traded like regular shares of stock.[2]

AMERICAN
DEPOSITARY
SHARE
(ADS)

A vehicle for foreign corporations to list their ordinary equity on an American stock exchange, such as the New York Stock Exchange or the NASDAQ.

Foreign corporations listed in other markets are not permitted to make direct secondary listings in the United States markets, thus this form of indirect ownership has been devised.

ADSs are US-dollar denominated and each share represents one or more underlying shares in the subject. These ADSs confer full rights of ownership (including dividends voting right) to these underlying shares, which are held on deposit by a custodian bank in the company's home country or territory.[3]

ASK (OFFER) PRICE

The lowest price a seller of a stock is willing to accept for a share of that given stock. For over-the-counter stocks, the asking price is the best quoted price at which a market maker is willing to sell a stock.[4]

AUDIT COMMITTEE

An operating committee of the Board of Directors charged with oversight of financial reporting and disclosure. Committee members are drawn from members of the company's board of directors, with a Chairperson selected from among the committee members.[5]

BEST EXECUTION

The obligation of an investment services firm (such as a stock broker) executing orders on behalf of customers to ensure that the prices those orders receive reflect the optimal mix of price improvement, speed and likelihood of execution. Brokers with customer orders are obligated to send orders to venues with the optimal "best execution stats."[6]

BID (OR BUY) PRICE

The price a market maker will buy a commodity at.[7]

BLOCK TRADE

A permissible, noncompetitive, privately

negotiated transaction either at or exceeding an exchange determined minimum threshold quantity of shares, which is executed apart and away from the open outcry or electronic markets. In the United States and Canada a block trade is usually at least 10,000 shares of a stock or $200,000 of bonds but in practice significantly larger.[8]

BLUE-SKY LAWS   A state law in the United States that regulates the offering and sale of securities to protect the public from fraud. Though the specific provisions of these laws vary among states, they all require the registration of all securities offerings and sales, as well as of stockbrokers and brokerage firms. Each state's blue sky law is administered by its appropriate regulatory agency, and most also provide private causes of action for private investors who have been injured by securities fraud.[9]

BROKER   An individual or party (brokerage firm) that arranges transactions between a buyer and a seller, and gets a commission when the deal is executed. A broker who also acts as a seller or as a buyer becomes a principal party to the deal.[10]

BROKER/DEALER   A natural person, a company or other organization that trades securities for its own account or on behalf of its customers.

Although many broker-dealers are "independent" firms solely involved in broker-dealer services, many others are business units or subsidiaries of commercial banks, investment banks or investment companies.

When executing trade orders on behalf of a customer, the institution is said to be acting as a *broker*. When executing trades for its own account, the institution is said to be acting as a *dealer*. Securities bought from clients or other firms in the capacity of dealer may be sold to clients or other firms acting again in the capacity of dealer, or they may become a part of the firm's holdings.[11]

CLEARING · The management of post-trading, pre-settlement credit exposures, to ensure that trades are settled in accordance with market rules, even if a buyer or seller should become insolvent prior to settlement.

Processes included in clearing are reporting/monitoring, risk margining, netting of trades to single positions, tax handling, and failure handling.[12]

COMMON STOCK · A form of corporate equity ownership, a type of security.[13]

CUSIP NUMBER · The 9-character alphanumeric CUSIP code identifies any North American security for the purposes of facilitating clearing and settlement of trades.[14]

DEPOSITARY · A bank organized in the United States which

BANK

provides all the stock transfer and agency services in connection with a depository receipt program. This function includes arranging for a custodian to accept deposits of ordinary shares, issuing the negotiable receipts which back up the shares, maintaining the register of holders to reflect all transfers and exchanges, and distributing dividends in U.S. dollars.[15]

DEPTH OF
MARKET

The size of an order needed to move the market a given amount. If the market is *deep*, a large order is needed to change the price. Market depth closely relates to the notion of liquidity, the ease to find a trading partner for a given order: a *deep* market is also a *liquid* market.[16]

DIRECT
PARTICIPATION
PROGRAM
(DPP)

A financial security that enables investors to participate in a business venture's cash flow and taxation benefits. Chiefly used in the past as a tax shelter, recent tax regulations have reduced its effectiveness in this respect.

DPP securities are traded on the OTC Bulletin Board since May 1997.

Direct participation programs are most commonly formed to invest in real estate, energy and equipment leasing projects.[17]

EDGAR

The *Electronic Data-Gathering, Analysis, and Retrieval* system, performs automated collection, validation, indexing, acceptance, and forwarding of submissions by companies and others who are required by law to file forms with the U.S. Securities and Exchange Commission (the "SEC"). The database is freely available to the public via the Internet (Web or FTP).[18]

EQUITY

The value of an ownership interest in property, including shareholders' equity in a business.[19]

FEDERAL RESERVE SYSTEM

The central banking system of the United States.[20]

FINRA

The *Financial Industry Regulatory Authority, Inc.*, or FINRA, is a private corporation that acts as a self-regulatory organization (SRO). FINRA is the successor to the *National Association of Securities Dealers, Inc.* (NASD). Though sometimes mistaken for a government agency, it is a non-governmental organization that performs financial regulation of member brokerage firms and exchange markets.[21]

INITIAL PUBLIC OFFERING (IPO)

A type of public offering where shares of stock in a company are sold to the general public, on a securities exchange, for the first time. Through this process, a private company transforms into a public company. Initial public offerings are used by companies to raise expansion capital, to possibly monetize the investments of early private investors, and to become publicly traded enterprises. A company selling shares is never required to repay the capital to its public investors.[22]

| INSTITUTIONAL INVESTOR | Organizations which pool large sums of money and invest those sums in securities, real property and other investment assets. They can also include operating companies which decide to invest their profits to some degree in these types of assets.[23] |

LEVEL I, II, III SUBSCRIPTIONS

NASDAQ quotes are available at three levels:
- Level 1 shows the highest bid and lowest offer—the inside quote.
- Level 2 shows all public quotes of market makers together with information of market dealers wishing to sell or buy stock and recently executed orders.
- Level 3 is used by the market makers and allows them to enter their quotes and execute orders.[24]

LIMIT ORDER

An order to buy a security at no more than a specific price, or to sell a security at no less than a specific price. This gives the trader (customer) control over the price at which the trade is executed; however, the order may never be executed ("filled"). Limit orders are used when the trader wishes to control price rather than certainty of execution.[25]

LIMIT ORDER PROTECTION (MANNING RULE)

A finance term based on the NASD regulation, NASD IM-2110-2.

The Manning Rule prohibits an NASD member firm from placing the firm's interest before/above the financial interests of a client.

For example, when a securities firm is holding a customer limit order (a limit order is an instruction to buy or sell securities at a certain price), the firm cannot ignore that order.

The firm cannot trade for their account using a price that would satisfy the customer's limit order without executing the customer limit order. The rule is applicable both in normal trading hours and in the extended hours trading sessions.[26]

LIQUIDITY — An asset's ability to be sold without causing a significant movement in the price and with minimum loss of value.[27]

MANNING RULE — See Limit Order Protection.

MARGIN — Collateral that the holder of a financial instrument has to deposit to cover some or all of the credit risk of their counterparty (most often their broker or an exchange). This risk can arise if the holder has done any of the following:
- borrowed cash from the counterparty to buy financial instruments,
- sold financial instruments short, or
- entered into a derivative contract.

The collateral can be in the form of cash or securities, and it is deposited in a *margin account*.[28]

MARKET — The total value of the tradable shares of

CAPITALIZATION — a publicly traded company; it is equal to the share price times the number of shares outstanding. As outstanding stock is bought and sold in public markets, capitalization could be used as a proxy for the public opinion of a company's net worth and is a determining factor in some forms of stock valuation. Preferred shares are not included in the calculation.[29]

MARKET MAKER — A company, or an individual, that quotes both a buy and a sell price in a financial instrument or commodity held in inventory, hoping to make a profit on the bid-offer spread, or turn.[30]

MARKET ORDER — A buy or sell order to be executed immediately at current market prices. As long as there are willing sellers and buyers, market orders are filled. Market orders are therefore used when certainty of execution is a priority over price of execution.[31]

NAKED SHORTING — Short-selling a tradable asset of any kind without first borrowing the security or ensuring that the security can be borrowed, as is conventionally done in a short sale. When the seller does not obtain the shares within the required time frame, the result is known as a "failure to deliver". The transaction generally remains open until the shares are acquired by the seller, or the seller's broker settles the trade.

Short selling is used to anticipate a price fall, but exposes the seller to the risk of a price rise.[32]

THE NASDAQ STOCK MARKET	The NASDAQ Stock Market, also known as simply the NASDAQ, is an American stock exchange. " NASDAQ" originally stood for "National Association of Securities Dealers Automated Quotations". It is the second-largest stock exchange by market capitalization in the world, after the New York Stock Exchange. As of January 25, 2011, there are 2,711 listings, with a total capitalization of over \$4.5 trillion. The NASDAQ has more trading volume than any other electronic stock exchange in the world. The exchange is owned by NASDAQ OMX Group, which also owns the OMX stock exchange network.[33]
THE NEW YORK STOCK EXCHANGE (NYSE)	The New York Stock Exchange, commonly referred to as the NYSE, is a stock exchange located at 11 Wall Street, Lower Manhattan, New York City, New York, United States. It is by far the world's largest stock exchange by market capitalization of its listed companies at US\$14.242 trillion as of Dec 2011. Average daily trading value was approximatelyUS\$153 billion in 2008.

The NYSE is operated by NYSE Euronext (NYSE: NYX), which was formed by the NYSE's 2007 merger with the fully electronic stock exchange Euronext.[34] |
| OVER-THE-COUNTER | *Over-the-counter (OTC)* or *off-exchange* trading is to trade financial instruments such as stocks, |

(OTC)	bonds, commodities or derivatives directly between two parties. It is contrasted with exchange trading, which occurs via facilities constructed for the purpose of trading (i.e. *exchanges*), such as futures exchanges or stock exchanges.[35]
OTCBB	A United States quotation medium for subscribing members used for many over-the-counter (OTC) equity securities that are not listed on the NASDAQ or a national stock exchange. Broker-dealers who subscribe to the system, which is not electronic, can use the OTCBB to enter orders for OTC securities that qualify to be quoted.[36]
PENNY STOCK	Common shares of small public companies that trade at less than $1.00. Penny stocks in the USA are often traded over-the-counter on the OTC Bulletin Board, or Pink Sheets. In the United States, both the Securities and Exchange Commission and FINRA have specific rules to define and regulate the sale of penny stocks.[37]
PINK SHEETS (OTC PINK)	A speculative trading marketplace that has no financial standards or reporting requirements. The stock of companies in the OTC Pink tier is not required to be registered with the SEC. Companies in this category are further categorized by the level and timeliness of information they provide to investors and may have current, limited or no public disclosure.[38]

PREFERRED
STOCK

An equity security with properties of both an equity and a debt instrument, and is generally considered a hybrid instrument. Preferreds are senior (i.e. higher ranking) to common stock, but subordinate to bonds in terms of claim (or rights to their share of the assets of the company).[39]

PROXY
STATEMENT

A statement required of a firm when soliciting shareholder votes. This statement is filed in advance of the annual meeting. The firm needs to file a proxy statement, otherwise known as a Form DEF 14A (Definitive Proxy Statement), with the U.S. Securities and Exchange Commission. This statement is useful in assessing how management is paid and potential conflict-of-interest issues with auditors. The statement includes:

- Voting procedure and information.
- Background information about the company's nominated directors including relevant history in the company or industry, positions on other corporate boards, and potential conflicts in interest.
- Board compensation.
- Executive compensation, including salary, bonus, non-equity compensation, stock awards, options, and deferred compensation. Also, information is included about perks such as personal use of company aircraft, travel, and tax gross-ups. Many companies will also include pre-determined payout packages for if an executive leaves the company.

- Who is on the audit committee, as well as a breakdown of audit and non-audit fees paid to the auditor.[40]

PUBLIC FLOAT

The number of outstanding shares in the hands of public investors as opposed to company officers, directors, or controlling-interest investors.[41]

ROUND LOT

A normal unit of trading of a security, which is usually 100 shares of stock. Any quantity less than this normal unit is referred to as an odd lot.[42]

SARBANES-OXLEY ACT OF 2002

A United States federal law that set new or enhanced standards for all U.S. public company boards, management and public accounting firms.

The act contains 11 titles, or sections, ranging from additional corporate board responsibilities to criminal penalties, and requires the Securities and Exchange Commission (SEC) to implement rulings on requirements to comply with the law.[43]

SECURITIES AND EXCHANGE COMMISSION (SEC)

A federal agency which holds primary responsibility for enforcing the federal securities laws and regulating the securities industry, the nation's stock and options exchanges, and other electronic securities markets in the United States. In addition to the Securities Exchange Act of 1934 that created it, the SEC enforces the Securities Act of 1933, the Trust Indenture Act of 1939, the

Investment Company Act of 1940, the Investment Advisers Act of 1940, the Sarbanes–Oxley Act of 2002 and other statutes. The SEC was created by Section 4 of the Securities Exchange Act of 1934 (now codified as 15 U.S.C. § 78d and commonly referred to as the 1934 Act).[44]

SETTLEMENT

A business process whereby securities or interests in securities are delivered, usually against (in simultaneous exchange for) payment of money, to fulfill contractual obligations, such as those arising under securities trades.

In the U.S., the settlement date for marketable stocks is usually 3 business days after the trade is executed, and for listed options and government securities it is usually 1 day after the execution.[45]

SHORT INTEREST RATIO (SIR)

A metric signaling prevailing investors' sentiment. The ratio is calculated by dividing the number of shares sold short by the average daily trading volume, generally over the last 30 trading days. The ratio represents the number of days it takes short sellers on average to repurchase all the borrowed shares. The ratio is used by both fundamental and technical traders to identify trends.

The short interest ratio can also be calculated for entire exchanges to determine the sentiment of the market as a whole. If an exchange has a high short interest ratio of around five or greater, this can be taken as a bearish signal, and vice versa.[46]

SHORT SALE

Short selling is the selling of a security that the seller does not own, or any sale that is completed by the delivery of a security borrowed by the seller. Such sales are made in anticipation of a decline in the price of the security to enable the seller to cover the sale with a purchase at a later date, at a lower price, and thus at a profit. Short sellers assume the risk that they will be able to buy the stock at a more favorable price than the price at which they sold short.

SHORT SQUEEZE

A short squeeze can occur if the price of stock with a high short interest begins to have increased demand and a strong upward trend. To cut losses, short sellers may add to demand by buying shares to cover short positions, causing the share price to further escalate temporarily. Short squeezes are more likely to occur in stocks with small market capitalization and a small public float.[47]

SPREAD

The difference in price between related securities.[48]

TRANSFER AGENT

Public companies typically use *transfer agents* to keep track of the individuals and entities that own their stocks and bonds. Most transfer agents are banks or trust companies, but sometimes a company acts as its own transfer agent.

Transfer agents perform three main functions:

1. Issue and cancel certificates to reflect changes in ownership. For example, when a company declares a stock dividend or stock split, the transfer agent issues new shares. Transfer agents keep records of who owns a company's stocks and bonds and how those stocks and bonds are held—whether by the owner in certificate form, by the company in book-entry form, or by the investor's brokerage firm in street name. They also keep records of how many shares or bonds each investor owns.

2. Act as an intermediary for the company. A transfer agent may also serve as the company's paying agent to pay out interest, cash and stock dividends, or other distributions to stock- and bondholders. In addition, transfer agents act as proxy agent (sending out proxy materials), exchange agent (exchanging a company's stock or bonds in a merger), tender agent (tendering shares in a tender offer), and mailing agent (mailing the company's quarterly, annual, and other reports).

3. Handle lost, destroyed, or stolen certificates. Transfer agents help shareholders and bondholders when a stock or bond certificate has been lost, destroyed, or stolen.[49]

VOLATILITY   A measure for variation of price of a financial instrument over time. Historic volatility is derived from time series of past market prices. An implied volatility is derived from the market price of a market traded derivative (in particular an option).[50]

VOLUME

In capital markets, *volume*, or *trading volume*, is the number of shares or contracts traded in a security or in an entire market during a given period of time.

In the context of stock trading on a stock exchange, the volume is commonly reported as the number of shares that changed hands during the day. Average volume is reported as the average volume over a longer period of time, normally one to three months. When the company appears in the news, the company's stock will usually deviate from its average volume, meaning that more people are trading this stock.[51]

[1] Glossary definitions made available by Wikimedia Foundation Inc. with attribution URLs for each definition appearing in the following Notes, under the Creative Commons Attribution/Share-Alike License; http://creativecommons.org/licenses/by-sa/3.0/

[2] http://en.wikipedia.org/wiki/American_depositary_receipt

[3] http://en.wikipedia.org/wiki/American_depositary_share

[4] http://en.wikipedia.org/wiki/Ask_price

[5] http://en.wikipedia.org/wiki/Audit_committee

[6] http://en.wikipedia.org/wiki/Best_execution

[7] http://en.wikipedia.org/wiki/Bid_(disambiguation)

[8] http://en.wikipedia.org/wiki/Block_trade

[9] http://en.wikipedia.org/wiki/Blue_sky_laws

[10] http://en.wikipedia.org/wiki/Broker

[11] http://en.wikipedia.org/wiki/Broker_dealer

[12] http://en.wikipedia.org/wiki/Clearing_(finance)

[13] http://en.wikipedia.org/wiki/Common_stock

[14] http://en.wikipedia.org/wiki/CUSIP_Number

[15] http://en.wikipedia.org/wiki/Depositary_bank

[16] http://en.wikipedia.org/wiki/Depth_of_market

[17] http://en.wikipedia.org/wiki/Direct_participation_program

[18] http://en.wikipedia.org/wiki/EDGAR

[19] http://en.wikipedia.org/wiki/Equity

[20] http://en.wikipedia.org/wiki/Federal_Reserve_System

[21] http://en.wikipedia.org/wiki/FINRA

[22] http://en.wikipedia.org/wiki/Initial_public_offering

[23] http://en.wikipedia.org/wiki/Institutional_investor

[24] http://en.wikipedia.org/wiki/NASDAQ#Quote_availability

[25] http://en.wikipedia.org/wiki/Limit_order#Limit_order

[26] http://en.wikipedia.org/wiki/Manning_rule

[27] http://en.wikipedia.org/wiki/Liquidity

[28] http://en.wikipedia.org/wiki/Margin_(finance)

[29] http://en.wikipedia.org/wiki/Market_capitalization

[30] http://en.wikipedia.org/wiki/Market_makers

[31] http://en.wikipedia.org/wiki/Market_order#Market_order

[32] http://en.wikipedia.org/wiki/Naked_shorting

[33] http://en.wikipedia.org/wiki/NASDAQ

[34] http://en.wikipedia.org/wiki/New_York_Stock_Exchange

[35] http://en.wikipedia.org/wiki/Over-the-counter_(finance)

[36] http://en.wikipedia.org/wiki/OTCBB

[37] http://en.wikipedia.org/wiki/Penny_Stock

[38] http://en.wikipedia.org/wiki/Pink_sheet#OTC_Pink

[39] http://en.wikipedia.org/wiki/Preferred_stock

[40] http://en.wikipedia.org/wiki/Proxy_statement

[41] http://en.wikipedia.org/wiki/Public_float

[42] http://en.wikipedia.org/wiki/Round_lot

[43] http://en.wikipedia.org/wiki/Sarbanes%E2%80%93Oxley_Act

[44] http://en.wikipedia.org/wiki/U.S._Securities_and_Exchange_Commission

[45] http://en.wikipedia.org/wiki/Settlement_(finance)

[46] http://en.wikipedia.org/wiki/Short_interest

[47] http://en.wikipedia.org/wiki/Short_interest

[48] http://en.wikipedia.org/wiki/Spread

[49] http://en.wikipedia.org/wiki/Transfer_agent

[50] http://en.wikipedia.org/wiki/Volatility_(finance)

[51] http://en.wikipedia.org/wiki/Volume_(finance)

www.ingramcontent.com/pod-product-compliance
Lightning Source LLC
Chambersburg PA
CBHW061830220326
41599CB00027B/5240